You're NOT Everyone's Cup of Tea — and That's OK!

by Trish Persen

You're NOT Everyone's Cup of Tea — and That's OK!

ISBN: 978-1-963980-14-1

Published by B-Global Publishing
©
2025

Orders from commercial bookstores and U.S. distributors:
Email support_staff@drbglobal.net

B-Global Publishing brings authors to your live events.
For more information or to book an event, contact
support_staff@drbglobal.net

Manufactured and printed in the United States of America and globally distributed by:
https://bglobalpublishing.drbglobal.net/

Author's Bio

Trish Persen is an educator, storyteller, and poetic truth-teller whose life's work is rooted in empowering others to own their narrative. With decades of experience guiding students in classrooms and hearts in conversation, Trish brings wisdom born of lived experience—intertwining the soul of a teacher with the vulnerability of a writer.

Known for her reflective voice and creative fire, she has spent her career encouraging students to find their own rhythm, write their own verses, and speak with clarity—even when their voices shake. Her work challenges perfectionism unpacks people-pleasing, and redefines success through self-awareness, compassion, and unapologetic authenticity.

Trish believes that we are all meant to take up space, to tell the truth of who we are—even when it doesn't fit into someone else's story. Through her writing, she reminds us that we're not here to be everyone's cup of tea—we're here to be our own.

She lives, writes, and teaches in Florida, where her backyard birds, a great playlist, and a good pen refill her soul.

Dedication

*For the ones who never **quite fit.***

*The **too much.***

*The **not enough.***

*The ones who **smile** in rooms that don't feel safe,
and **shrink** to make **others** comfortable.*

*You were **never** meant to be everyone's **cup of tea.**
And what a **sacred relief** that is.*

This is for you.

*May you **remember who you are**,
without apology.*

Introduction
Let's Get One Thing Straight

 *You are NOT everyone's cup of tea.*

TRISH PERSEN

Introduction - Let's Get One Thing Straight

You are NOT everyone's cup of tea.

This is a metaphor for life.

This book invites you to be bold enough to take ownership of your identity. *Know Thyself*—or *Nosce te ipsum* (Latin)—is a philosophical maxim that has been embedded in my brain before I could talk. I did not come to really "knowing" this concept until reflected through my studies as an undergrad of English Literature. Subjected to many philosophers throughout my educational journey, it was Socrates that resonated with my own spirit the most. He believed that understanding oneself is the foundation for acquiring other knowledge and making responsible choices. This essentially became a philosophical commandment emphasizing the importance of introspection and self-awareness. Who we are lies in the power within us all.

The problem that we face as human beings is the constant search for validation outside of ourselves. This begins at the onset of first life. The doctor "spanks" our bottoms for us to realize we are no longer in the womb and exist outside of it. Our realities become modeled in external stimuli. The measurement of accomplishment or failure is reliant on a parent's love (or lack thereof), the number of friends you have, grades on a report card, or a symbolic "checklist" of the tasks that NEED to get done. There are so many things to list, but it is these self-sabotaging limitations that often leave us feeling unfulfilled even in the highest points of our timelines.

We have this internal limitation believing that if we just "people please" enough all will be right in the world. What we become blinded to realize is that we do this at the expense of our own happiness. There is the illusion that if we make others happy, that will make us happy. This statement was always true for me—so I thought…

It genuinely fills my soul to make someone else smile. I love paying attention to the people I relate to and noticing the "little things" that bring them joy. However, this vibration could immediately get clouded once you start internalizing how it is being received. It is a human condition to seek validation. Our intention is pure, but it is easy to fall back on the desire to be validated. This sets us up for disappointment.

Making others smile is a positive vibration, but sometimes we are depleting our energies on people that may never truly receive it the way we want them to. This is a harsh reality that I had to face many times on my own journey, but there is hope. We need to learn how to "Flip the Script" or—one of my personal favorites—Shift Your Narrative.

Knowing Thyself is knowing that ***You are NOT everyone's cup of tea*** and that is **OK.**

Chapter ONE

Know Thyself

> *Shakespeare is not everyone's cup of tea, neither was I.*
>
> TRISH PERSEN

Chapter One: Know Thyself

Shakespeare is not everyone's cup of tea, neither was I.

As a lifelong learner, I came to realize this concept early on. I feel that it is this knowing led me to become an educator. I had this innate desire to want everyone to see the value in understanding each other. It took a long time and several planning periods in tears to realize ultimately; I did not have the power I thought I had. I thought I would be able to change every student that crossed my path. Gift them with an undeniable perspective that would change their course of life indefinitely for the better. I could not be any more naïve...

While in school to get the degree to become a teacher, you are subjected to philosophy, pedagogy, and papers. The trifecta of this experience leaves many with a heart filled with hope and purpose. You feel armed with all the essential tools to help educate the next generation and create an army of successful people that will do good in the world. This is worn as a badge of honor for all to see. It was an amazing feeling to absorb all the gems of those that came before you, feeding your soul with indescribable emotions, and a promising outlook of the future. This was going to be everything you ever wanted, and you would define yourself as an "Educator" for the rest of your life. All would be right in the world.

The problem with seeing a future through rose-colored glasses is that you miss checking yourself first. The disappointment comes on fast and swift. It is nothing like you have ever felt before. You quickly become defined by how your students are behaving, how much they are learning, or even if they are interested in the first place. This becomes how you measure your success. You could have a classroom full of 30 students and most are engaged, but it is those handful sleeping that will take a hold on you like the grudge an Italian grandmother has held for over 30 years with her sister.

That handful of sleeping students will fester in your brain as a continued reminder of failure. You will cry into your lesson plan books and have a tear-stained desk calendar for the entire school year if this is not reconciled in your head. This was my reality for the first year of teaching high school. It would surface again throughout my career, but I had an awareness now when met with the challenge. These stories will be threaded throughout this book, but for now I will focus on this one.

I was going to change the world by educating students with my love of philosophy and Shakespeare. Just as Shakespeare is not everyone's cup of tea, neither was I. I could not fathom this concept, and it was the bane of my existence for quite some time. I could not get over the fact that I did not have everyone's full attention and all this amazing knowledge I had in my head was not transferring to everyone.

"How could you not love poetry? —

The Bard does nothing for you? —

Chaucer is a genius, what's the matter with you?"

Defeated thoughts on the daily would enter my head. Questioning EVERYTHING was a familiar routine at this time. I was entering a downward spiral --- fast. I contemplated quitting so many times (confession: this would not be the last time…), but then I had a "check-in" with my English Department head. She sat me down and wanted to get a pulse on how things were going. I was beat up and could not control my emotions. She immediately saw the welling in my eyes and heard the cracks in my voice. She proceeded very firm, "You do not cry—*they* cry!" I was taken aback at first. My whole MO was that I would reach every student and prove that I care. Seeing the look of shock on my face, she explained that I was hired for my heart and drive, but I should never let any one of them take that from me.

She stated things like, "You worked hard to get here — You have the knowledge — You have control — We serve to educate, NOT to be well liked…"

Having a decade of experience over me, I trusted her. She allowed me to realize that it was okay to have the passion I did, and it was okay for not everyone to like it. I also realized that I needed to have more than just book smarts when it came to this relationship. We often define our roles in life as what they are "on paper," negating the fact that there are layers to every aspect of what makes you, *you*. I had forgotten my time in a former life as a DJ when I had to lean in and LISTEN to my audience. Sure, I had all the tracks, the skill, and personality, but is that what the crowd truly wanted? Not entirely. It was in this reflection that I discovered my ability to adjust. There is a strong example of this ability to adjust that I often use now to illustrate to my college-level students how to adapt when it comes to different audience types. It goes a little something like this…

The year was 2009 (give or take a year), and I taught 6 out of 7 periods of 12th Grade English. My 6th period was special. The entire class was male. Wait, before you get all hostile and call me a sexist, this did not faze me one bit. Most of my cousins were male, and many of the neighbors' kids were male. I was very comfortable in this environment. The special thing about this group was they happened to be members of the football team. Again, stop jumping down my throat. The dilemma at hand was that I was about to teach my Shakespearean unit. Just think about that for a moment and be truthful about the answer to my next question. In all honesty, do you believe the football team had any interest in learning/reading Shakespeare? The answer should be a resounding NO; however, if you need more proof I will give it to you.

First day of the new unit, naïve Trish believes she will crush the statistics and get this class on board. I was terribly mistaken and was met with grunts and growls followed by naps with drool-soaked desks. Needless to say, I went home very defeated and had no idea how I was going to get through this unit successfully—especially with 6th period. With my head in my hands, my brain hurt trying to come up with ways—and then all of a sudden it hit me square in the face! "I know FOOTBALL!" Ever since I was able to hold up my own head (maybe before then), I watched the game with my dad. He taught me everything there was to know about the game. This would later be used to his amusement as he would watch the boys' jaws drop while I would give a play-by-play of the games. The icing on the cake for this doting father was telling the boys, "She is awesome, isn't she… but you can't date her!" He got a kick out of that and it's one of my fondest memories that I will cherish forever. I digress…

Back to our dilemma: I had this revelation. I knew their language! The next day I went in with my head held high and hope in my heart. 6th period came and I greeted them at the door like always and of course the question, "Are we still doing Shakespeare, Mrs. P?" was asked, followed by an eye-roll and yawn. I just nodded my head with a small noticeable smirk on my face. The bell rang and I did not start off with the elements of a Shakespearean play, I chose to start out with a conversation about last Friday's game against the Mustangs (Merritt Island HS football team). Here is how it went:

"Afternoon! Wow! Friday night's game was spectacular!"
"You were there, Mrs. P?"
"Of course I was, I love football!... Exciting game! You guys were down in the third and then Jake caught that interception to run it back for 6 points!"
"Yeah!" the whole classroom fills with cheers and then Jake adds, "Yeah! That turned the whole game around! We ended up winning!"
"It was truly amazing to watch and celebrate with you — You know what else is awesome? That is what you call a *turning point*." [drops the mic]

It took them a few seconds to realize what happened, but then the light bulbs went off over each head. It was a victory in my book—and in theirs. The confidence that came after that, not only for me, but in them, was astounding. They finally realized that they had the power to understand and did not have to "live up" to the football player label. This was worth celebrating all by itself, but I kid you not, when it came to the final battle between Macduff and Macbeth, they moved the desks out of the way to act it out!

Are all instances going to be as triumphant as this? No, but it is not the outcome that you have to be fixated on—it is the act of being *you* and utilizing everything you have captive in your toolbox to stay authentic to your spirit. Remember: you only have control over how it makes *you* feel.

Sometimes connection does not just rely on what you can understand, but the understanding of how others can understand. Stepping outside of yourself and perspective is hard. It is a subconscious ego thing, and we believe the disconnect is all about us. That is where the self-doubt rears its ugly head. When in essence it is beyond our perception of who we are. Understanding that outside perception is out of our control. Once we make the decision to show up as we are it takes time to acknowledge, but once we do, it is the most freeing experience we can ever have. We can only be responsible for the pursuit of our own happiness. When we are in our element and professing what lights us up, we are in flow. In that flow, our vibration is at the highest it will ever possibly be. Your audience will either be attracted to the vibration and crave what you are gifting, or it will be too much for them and they will turn away from it. Wherever the frequency lands, the most important home is you.

It is crazy how we do not see past our own nose sometimes and we create this reality of things based on how we believe they should be or outcomes that are beyond our own control. I had the power to bring this knowledge to the table and present it as such, but I did not have the power over how it is received. Literature was my bag, and not everyone carries a Coach.

I knew I would not survive the year if I did not absorb the words of my mentor. I needed to truly reflect on what makes me happy and motivated to move forward. Digging deeper into reflection and finding the power that has always been there. As you can tell from the example, this is not a one-time thing, and it will come up again and again over time. This is to remind us of that power. Once I started to release any hang-up on outcomes outside of remembering my own joy when it came to the subject matter, I started to find that spark again. When you rediscover that fire inside of you, *you* remember who you are. That fire will translate to your audience. Those who will resonate will recognize it right away, become engaged, and those that don't—won't.

For a teacher, this is not only difficult on a personal level, but a professional one as well. The measurement of student engagement and success is attached to our journey whether we like it or not. It is our business to continue to try to reach as many students as we can. The secret sauce is becoming the reflection for them to figure out their responsibility for their own success. Just as we as educators must take ownership of our role in this partnership, they do as well. Success does not always have to be measured in academics, there are triumphs in getting students to realize their individual responsibility. This is not an easy task and may take some of them a lifetime to figure out, but that is something I had to let go of.

Trish…You are just not everyone's cup of tea and that is ok.

✦ Reflection Questions – Chapter 1 ✦

You're Not Everyone's Cup of Tea...and That's Okay

Before you turn the page, take a quiet moment with yourself. This chapter opened the door to understanding how we show up in a world that doesn't always understand us—and how that's not only okay, but necessary. Reflection helps you process, uncover patterns, and—most importantly—step into the truth of who you are.

Here are a few questions to sit with before you continue:

1. When was the first time you felt misunderstood or misread by someone else? How did you respond, and what did it teach you about how others perceive you?

2. Whose approval are you still seeking, even unconsciously? What might change in your life if you released that need?

3. Have you ever changed part of yourself to be more "palatable" to others? What did that cost you emotionally, creatively, or spiritually?

4. If you could give your younger self one truth about being "not everyone's cup of tea," what would it be? And are you ready to fully believe it now?

Chapter TWO

Validation is a Trap

This is not "fitting in" this is an allusion through the "safety" of conformity.

TRISH PERSEN

Chapter Two: Validation is a Trap

This is not "fitting in" this is an allusion through the "safety" of conformity.

Validation is a human condition that everyone falls victim to. Even the most successful, confident people in the world have moments of vulnerability that expose them to this fallacy. Social media is the strongest example of how thirsty we are for it. However, one does not look at it that way when it comes to social media. We tell ourselves we are doing it for our friends and family back home, for business visibility, to build relationships. This may be part of the motivation, but let's be real—we are looking for someone to validate the "importance" of our existence.

We often need the like or the comment to make the experience "more real," instead of feeling the moment, reflecting on what emotions the experience evokes on the inside. Somehow what an outside person says about the experience we share overrides the truth of the experience. Our memory of the experience becomes clouded by outside perspectives with their own emotions attached. The story changes as each comment reveals how "we should" feel about the experience. The results are often the same. No matter which way we look at it, there is a justification for it. It gives us this false sense of security. A sense that we are not alone. This is not "fitting in"—this is an illusion through the "safety" of conformity. It is a drug—the more validation we receive, positive or negative, the hunger grows stronger for the next time. We lose track of who we truly are without it.

This behavior does not just come out of nowhere. It is wonderful when we are validated on a positive tip, but the majority of the time it is for a negative action. We feed off the attention and feel that the more controversial, the more attention. We often lose sight of our inner purpose in the first place. We learn this very early on in life.

I give you a simple, but deep layered example. When we are a child and do not have the ability to place linguistics with the sounds we are making, we learn by mimicking. Mainly from the "adults" in our lives. The problem with this is, as "adults" we often dismiss the weight of the words we say and brush them off as the child doesn't understand—it won't matter. So we go about our adult life spewing cuss words whenever we feel like it without a care in the world until one day your two-year-old says: **FUCK.**

The initial reaction is not of shock—NO—it's a belly laugh that comes projecting out like your favorite comic just gave the punch line of a lifetime. In this fit of laughter, your toddler feeds off the high vibration of laughter and reads it as approval (validation of a good deed) and says it again—**FUCK.** Some adults will not be able to control themselves and continue to laugh and this becomes a validation of behavior. Your toddler catches the vibration, and it makes them "feel good" they are making you laugh. The addiction begins.

There is comfort in the feeling that you are making others comfortable. This is a battle that I have navigated through my whole life. We morph into this "people-pleasing monster" often at our own expense. There is this belief if we conform to what others have conformed to, there will be peace in the conformity and sense of contentment. The problem with contentment—especially when it is for the sake of others—we lose our inner peace.

This is a silly example, but one I believe will help paint the picture of how this could be harmful to your inner spirit. I was one that loved to dress. Although we did not have the money to go designer, my mom taught me how to be savvy at thrift stores to put outfits together. I could not wait to wear my newest shirt or blazer. It made me feel good. I felt like this made me present. I was ready every day and was excited about learning. This did not make me popular, but I did not change who I was and continued to get "called out" every day. So be it!

When we are questioning and feel lost, this does not mean we are absent from knowing who we are. This is a temporary deflection. It is another part of the process for us. It is a reminder that to continue to learn and grow, there will always be questions to ask ourselves—always. The feeling of confusion or being in the state of feeling lost is a nudge from the universe that we need to dive deeper. Or we have been letting something that stifled us before get in the way of our progress.

We allow this to happen because we did not take 100% ownership of what was holding us back in the first place. Some will call this "passing the buck." The language that we are using is the language that we have used in the past to justify unsavory actions. It is easy to defer any responsibility of this stifled state by blaming others for the cause of it. We can also lose ourselves in getting the validation of this deflection on a common ground company that has shared the same scapegoat. This is a disastrous union, as you have entered a relationship of justifying the unsavory actions of both parties by giving the only reason why it occurs was because of some outside entity.

This becomes so dangerous as the personal responsibility becomes non-existent. When this happens the motivation to reflect dissipates. There is no longer a desired need to explore within because at this state the problem has been resolved by deflecting. This cycle will continue even if there are moments of coming back to the reality of the situation. To break this cycle, you have to remember that no one knows you better than you.

Looking for validation from someone that is just as lost as you will keep you in the state of the unrecognizable. When it comes down to it, you already know the answers to the questions within but make the choice to ignore your own intuition for someone else to make your actions OK for you. That does not mean we cannot ask for help or guidance from the outside—but understand YOU first. Recognize the genuine person or people that will help you back to reflection. A person or a people with a personal agenda or somehow making it about their personal conflicts does not have your best interest at heart. They may not even know that they are doing this because it is temporarily filling a need for validation in their own circumstances.

Getting angry for this manipulation would be the same as getting angry with yourself for the same instance. What makes the difference is the anger towards yourself will indicate that you are now aware and ready to reflect. You are now ready to resolve the issue for your own spirit and look at it with hyper clarity.

Having this awareness will save you from a world of the wrong kind of pain. The kind of pain that stays stagnant at a dull hum throughout your life, creating a constant stream of unresolved depression and anxiety that you cannot explain. We are human—this will happen in our lifetime, there is no question. It is how we come to be aware of when it is happening and learn the lesson. We need to sit with our shadows before we can see the light of another day. This is what is fact. This is what is reality. There is light, there is darkness, and then there is light again.

Anything on the outside of you is the reality from the story that we are creating in our own minds. When we are confused or lost, the reality gets distorted; we manifest what we are thinking. If we allow these outside forces to dictate what we think and feel, then what we think and feel will become what we see. If we are not careful, this could become our permanent reality—secured by those that wish to get lost in the same reality where all is justified and responsibility is deflected.

We are the only ones that have the power to change that perception. No one else knows YOU better than YOU. Recognize those that feel compelled to tell you who you are. Recognize those claiming that you are the same and experience things the same way. No one experiences things the same way. There may be similarities, yes, but YOU are YOU and THEY are THEY. There is no other way.

If we were all meant to be the same, we would be. We are not. That is what we need to realize as a collective species. We are from the same God or gods (depending on the belief system) that are ALL and EVERYTHING. Wisdom is infinite. One mortal human being could not possibly possess everything. That is why we are not the same and are meant to exchange that wisdom with each other.

Once we realize this and reflect on who we truly are, validation from the outside is no longer needed and we are free. The notion that we are not everyone's cup of tea is the only validation that we need to move forward. We no longer need to attach ourselves to anyone or anything to define who and what we are.

But how did I get here? Why did I feel I had to be everyone's favorite in the first place?

That is what this journey is all about, and I will continue to illustrate that as you navigate through mine.

✦ Reflection Questions – Chapter 2 ✦

As you've explored in this chapter, the search for validation—whether through titles, praise, or the approval of others—can be both seductive and deceiving. It's human to want to be seen and celebrated, but true grounding comes from within. We often chase validation as if it's the ultimate reward, only to find that its shine fades quickly without internal peace and self-assurance. Recognizing that external validation is fleeting while self-worth is enduring is a powerful turning point. You've learned here that it's not only okay to want to be seen—it's okay to do the seeing for yourself first.

Reflection Questions:

1. When have you found yourself chasing external validation, and how did it feel when you got it—or didn't?

2. What parts of yourself are you still waiting for someone else to approve of?

3. In what ways can you begin validating your own efforts, talents, or growth today?

4. What would it look like to move through your life knowing that your worth doesn't depend on applause?

Chapter THREE
The Crash

...the crash isn't the end. It's the moment you realize your worth was never theirs to define.

TRISH PERSEN

Chapter Three: The Crash

...the crash isn't the end. It's the moment you realize your worth was never theirs to define.

We all come to crossroads in our lives—pivotal moments where what we believed to be true no longer fits. Sometimes, these moments are subtle. Other times, they slap us awake. We may live under the illusion that we belong, that we are valued, and act accordingly. But often, it's just that—an illusion.

So, my friends, I've told you about those disillusioning moments — the ones where you think you're in the right place, doing all the right things, and for a while, it even feels like everything is perfect. You ignore the doubts. You convince yourself that everyone is aligned with you, that you're truly seen. And then... people reveal themselves. Their real selves. And it hurts. You're disappointed. You're heartbroken.

We all have those moments. But then there are the ones that hit harder — the ones that are so undeniably clear, so in-your-face, that you can't pretend anymore. You know without a doubt: you are *not* their cup of tea. And no matter what you do, no matter how good your intentions, you feel the disapproval. You feel the rejection. Still, some part of you pushes forward. Your inner spirit refuses to lie down. You just keep going.

I have a story like that. One of the most devastating seasons of my life. I was finishing the literature part of my undergraduate degree and entering the education program. I knew I wanted to be a teacher. Service had always been in my heart. I had considered the medical field — maybe a doctor or veterinarian — but I knew I couldn't do it. My heart was too tender. I would lose my very first patient and never recover. But children? I could do something there. I wanted to be part of their world, especially the little ones.

Elementary school had always held a kind of magic for me. I was a small, quiet kid, but I loved school. I loved my teachers. They were warm, kind, full of light. I wanted to be that for someone else. So naturally, I chose the elementary school track, and when it came time for student teaching, I was thrilled to be placed in a kindergarten class. I was juggling work, school, and side jobs, but I was doing it. I wasn't alone — lots of people grind through school like that. Thankfully, the jobs I had supported my education, and I made it work.

Before that placement even began, I remember meeting with my education advisor. She told me flat-out: "You shouldn't have a full-time job. You shouldn't have a boyfriend. Honestly, you shouldn't have too many friends. This program is your life now."

I was already living on my own. Paying my own way. I had no choice — not really. I don't fault my parents. My mom got the call when I was 17 that I was aging out of benefits and had one year to figure it out. So, I did. I figured it out. Even if that meant sleeping in my car or couch-hopping to finish school, I was going to do it. I smiled politely at my advisor and thought, "Maybe you have a cot in the basement, then."

Once my classes began, I was fully immersed. I was in a senior thesis course for my English degree — a passion project on Greek tragedy — and I was thriving. I wrote about Antigone. I was nerding out, deeply in love with the material. My professor was a playwright and totally invested in our learning. That class was a gift, even though it met late and I was exhausted half the time.

My education classes were going well too. All A's — until one class. "Lesson Planning and Strategies." This class was connected directly to my student teaching in kindergarten, and I had a great relationship with my cooperating teacher. The kids adored her. They adored me. I got to read with them, sit on the floor with them, paint, draw, sing. It was everything I had imagined.

One of our first assignments in class was to create a lesson plan. I used inspiration from the library visit I had with the kindergarteners — a display of Aesop's Fables. I remembered how, as a child, those stories helped me learn right from wrong. I was excited. I drafted the lesson, reviewed it with my mentor teacher, and got her enthusiastic stamp of approval.

I handed it in with confidence. A week passed. I was back in the classroom with the kids, the teacher cheering me on, when I got the graded assignment back. It was covered in red ink.

And not just feedback — judgment.

"You will never be a teacher," she wrote.

I sat stunned. She tore apart my language. Claimed kindergartners wouldn't understand what fables were. That Aesop was too advanced. But it wasn't just a critique. It was a dismissal of who I was and what I brought. I later found out she was a principal from a district far out on the island. She was impossible to reach and barely approachable in class.

That should have been my cue to go to my advisor. To drop the class. But I didn't. I stayed.

Then came our next major assignment — an in-class presentation. I had everything prepared: laminated visuals, an organized agenda, professional attire. The other students — God bless them — were in messy buns and sweatpants, reading off of torn notebook paper. But still, I was the one who got points deducted. For "organization." For "professionalism." I received a C. It didn't add up.

She clearly had a problem with me. And to this day, I honestly don't know why. You'd think I showed up late or disrespected her. I didn't. I showed up early, dressed sharp, overprepared. And yet, her energy toward me never shifted. I just wasn't her cup of tea.

It gets harder here.

Two weeks before the semester ended, my father passed away.

He had been one of my biggest fans. On Tuesdays, after student teaching, I used to visit him at the rehab center where he stayed due to complications from MS. He'd light up when he saw me. Compliment my outfits. Ask about my classes. He was proud.

The night he went to the hospital, I was in my thesis class. We were presenting our papers creatively, and I had written a poem: *"The Apple Doesn't Fall Far from the Tree."* It was about Antigone and her father, and unknowingly, it had become a tribute to mine. My professor asked me where my writing came from, and I told him — about my mom teaching me to write poems using spelling words, and my dad singing Motown while I danced around the living room. That was my foundation.

He didn't know my dad. But when he found out he had passed, he came to the funeral. He told me, "I felt like I knew him through you."

I'll never forget that.

I didn't tell anyone else. Not at school. I didn't want pity. I wanted to finish strong, because that's what my dad would have wanted. I was the first in my family to even be close to graduating. I needed to finish the last two weeks.

While I was still grieving — quietly — I got called into the education office. My advisor told me they were "concerned about my future in the program." She said I was failing my Teaching Strategies class.

I was stunned.

How could I be failing when my final projects weren't even due yet? I was getting A's in every other class — including my senior thesis. But this professor had already made up her mind. My advisor told me to "give myself grace," attributing the grade drop to my father's passing.

I stopped her.

"I'm not using my father's death as an excuse," I said. "And I'd appreciate it if no one else did, either."

She offered condolences. But the damage was done. The story had been written for me.

In our final class session, I was with the other girls — the same ones who gave their presentations in sweats with scribbled notes — and I asked about their grades. They got perfect scores. Meanwhile, I had been docked for "lack of professionalism."

That was the moment I *knew*.

I went into the room for my final meeting with the professor. She offered her condolences too, and then said it:

"Some people just aren't cut out for this. Not everyone gets through."

I thanked her. With bile in my throat.

But here I am. Over a decade later. Still teaching. Still thriving. Still here.

Because what she couldn't see in me, I *refused* to let die in myself.

I made it — not the way I first imagined, but I made it. And still, it didn't come without another heartbreak.

I always told myself it was worth it. I'd look at the outcome — the beautifully decorated prom, the joy of Homecoming, the energy of the powder puff game — and say, "Look at how happy everyone is. Look at what we built. This matters." I told myself I was doing the right thing. That everyone loved it. That I belonged. I was Miss Persen, after all. People knew me.

And so I kept going. I shut out the noise — the warnings, the kind suggestions from others to slow down. "You're going to burn out," they said. "You're doing too much." But I didn't listen.

And then something happened.

I got called into a meeting. It was during a time when the school was facing major budget cuts. Many of us were already teaching six out of seven periods — a brutal load. I was one of the teachers who volunteered to give up a planning period. That hour was supposed to be for prep, grading, resetting — but I gave it up willingly, because I was also sponsoring the student government, the senior class, and organizing countless events. That "free" period was usually spent in meetings, covering for other teachers, or catching my breath in passing.

We were stretched thin, but we told ourselves we were doing it for each other. For our students. For the good of the community. And still — it wasn't enough.

At that meeting, there was a whiteboard. My name was on it, under a list that said: *"Teachers who don't teach FCAT."* For anyone who doesn't know, FCAT was Florida's standardized test system at the time. Certain grades didn't participate — and 12th grade, the grade I taught, was one of them.

I taught 12th grade English because I had been asked to take on our very first senior class. No books, no curriculum, no precedent. Just a chance to build something from scratch. I was excited. I spent an entire summer preparing — because that's just who I am. It was a creative challenge, and I dove in.

But because I didn't "teach the test," I wasn't seen as essential in the eyes of the district. That was the reality. While other teachers saw me as hardworking, while students saw me as supportive and consistent — the data didn't support my value. I wasn't seen as relevant.

It was crushing.

They needed English teachers, yes, but the plan was to collapse my classes into others — reassign students, redistribute schedules. I wouldn't lose my job, necessarily. But I'd lose *my home*. That school *was* my home. My colleagues were my family. I had built that senior class from the ground up. I was there before anyone, left after everyone, volunteered my weekends, showed up without complaint.

And now, my name was on a board under a title that read like a dismissal.

My heart broke.

I couldn't wrap my head around it. I sat there thinking, *How am I only being seen through this one metric? What about the dances? The fundraisers? The nights I stayed late so my students could feel seen, heard, celebrated?*

That meeting was a wake-up call. A brutal one.

I realized that no matter how valuable you *feel*, it can all shift in a moment — and suddenly, you're no longer seen as essential. You're just... extra. Unnecessary. It doesn't matter that you gave your heart. The system sees data, not devotion.

I told myself to keep it together. I told myself it was just a possibility, not a certainty. But it hovered. That heartbreak lingered in the background of every school day. It sat with me in my classroom. And even though I tried to mask it, my students could feel it.

Three of my girls — students I taught, but also worked with through Student Government — came to me after class.

"Mrs. P... are you okay?"

I smiled my usual smile, gave them my upbeat, nothing-to-see-here voice. "Yeah, I'm great! It's Friday, we've got the weekend ahead. I'm great."

But they shook their heads.

"You're not the same."

That hit me harder than the meeting. Harder than seeing my name on that board.

Because I thought I was hiding it. I thought I could keep my heartbreak separate from my teaching, keep my students protected from what I was feeling. But they saw me. And in that moment, I knew — I couldn't stay.

It was the beginning of the end.

As positive as I am, I knew I had to make a move. But leaving wasn't easy. I wasn't just shifting classrooms — I was shifting my entire identity. I made the decision not to move laterally, but forward — into higher education, where I could be creative again, where I could breathe, where I could rebuild.

Even then, when I told my principal I was leaving, I got hit with doubt. "What if it doesn't work out?" "You'll lose your professional certificate." I was already certified. I had tenure. But fear has a funny way of disguising itself as practicality.

Still, I left.

And over a decade later, I'm still here — thriving in postsecondary education.

I made the right choice. But the lesson? It came back.

Because even in new spaces, we repeat old patterns. I became the "yes" person again. Took on more. Volunteered. Overcommitted. And just like before, I burned the candle at both ends, thinking I had to prove myself all over again.

And then, once again, I found myself in a place where all my effort, all my giving, suddenly didn't count. It was about what I could do *next* — not what I had already done.

That's the part that stings. When you realize that your loyalty, your labor, your love — it's conditional in the eyes of systems that measure worth in productivity.

So, I'm here now, telling you: give yourself some grace.

Understand that some lessons will come back around. Some heartbreaks echo. But you are not the same version of yourself each time. And if you're paying attention, you'll respond differently.

You may be someone's cup of tea for a season, and then you're not. And that's okay.

It hurts. Absolutely. But knowing who you are — knowing what you've built, what you've given, who you've lifted — that doesn't go away just because someone else stops seeing it.

Everything you've done still happened. Everything you've created still matters. And the people you've touched? Some of them stay with you for life.

To this day, I still hear from students in that first senior class. I've been to their weddings, their baby showers, their college celebrations. I've watched them grow. And I wouldn't trade that for anything. Sometimes, the crash isn't the end. It's the moment you realize your worth was never theirs to define. Some relationships are forever. Some are for a season. And that's okay.

✦ Reflection Questions – Chapter 3 ✦

This chapter—*The Crash*—brought us to that raw, pivotal place where the illusion shatters, and the truth about how we're perceived comes crashing down. This chapter shared a deeply personal story of heartbreak, rejection, and perseverance in the face of dismissal. But within the wreckage, a different kind of strength emerged—the kind that comes when you're no longer willing to shrink or contort yourself for approval. "The Crash" wasn't just about hitting the bottom; it was about choosing to rise differently, with clarity and ownership of your truth. It was the moment you realized that not being someone's cup of tea wasn't a tragedy—it was a kind of freedom.

Reflection Questions:

1. Can you recall a time in your life when someone's rejection made you question your path or your worth? What did you learn from it?

2. How do you typically respond when someone makes you feel "not good enough"? Do you shrink, fight, overcompensate—or pause and reflect?

3. What beliefs about yourself were "written in red ink" by someone else? Are you ready to rewrite them?

4. What has "the crash" taught you about your capacity to rebuild—not the same, but stronger and more grounded?

Chapter FOUR
Flipping the Script

*It's how I heal.
It's not
performative.
It's my
resistance.*

TRISH PERSEN

Chapter Four: Flipping the Script

It's how I heal. It's not performative. It's my resistance.

Christopher Wallace, aka Biggie Smalls, once said, *"Turned negative into a positive — that's the life I live."* That lyric got under my skin back in the '90s, and it never really left. Back then, I was just coming of age, trying to figure out the rhythm of life. The world felt too big, too uncertain, but that line made sense to me. It still does. It's truth disguised as a beat.

But flipping the script isn't easy — especially when we're surrounded by fear, doubt, and the constant whispers of limitation. It's easy to fall into the negative, to make a home out of it because it's familiar. The pain, the blocks, the spiral — they can feel strangely comforting because at least we *know* them. They validate our worst fears. But somewhere in that cycle, a quiet voice begins to stir, asking: *what if this isn't it?*

Like many of the moments you've already read, I've had choices. So many. Stay stuck or move. Stay silent or speak. Sit in the dark or open the blinds. And let me be clear — I don't believe we should push past sadness, or frustration, or the weight of depression. You have to *feel* those things. You have to sit in them long enough to understand your way out. The only way out is through.

I think back to my undergrad years — where the struggle wasn't just academic. It was financial. It was personal. It was emotional. I shared a glimpse of this in the last chapter, but the truth is, it ran deeper. I wasn't just learning in school. I was learning in life. About rejection. About worth. About what it meant to keep going when every door slammed shut.

I came from a military family — my father was a Vietnam vet — and yet, no Pell Grant. No help. I was told my stepmother's income was too high to qualify, though we didn't have enough to stretch. On the other side, my stepfather's income would've been counted too. Either way, it didn't add up to support. So I had to find other ways.

That meant working full-time, going to school full-time, and taking on weekend gigs — DJing, cocktail waitressing, you name it. And right after I finally got everything aligned to register for classes, two weeks in, I was in a major car accident. It felt like the universe kept handing me bricks while asking me to swim.

At first, I blamed all the outside circumstances. No car. No help. No cushion. Just one blow after another. But eventually, I realized something I wasn't ready to admit before: **the biggest obstacle was me.** My thinking. My spiral. My refusal to believe there was a way forward. I had accepted the story that the world was against me.

That's when the idea of flipping the script became more than a lyric. It became a lifeline.

I didn't quit school. Even when I was treated unfairly by a professor who seemed to dismiss me before I even spoke — I didn't fold. I didn't walk out with a dramatic exit. I regrouped. I took a beat. And then I changed direction.

My father, who had passed not long before, was always proud of me. He believed in my strength even when I didn't. My mother did too — always encouraging my creativity, always reminding me that I was more than the struggle. So I made a decision.

I returned to my English Literature degree. Writing had always been my first love. Language is where I thrive. It wasn't an escape — it was a homecoming.

Then, an unexpected door opened. I was offered the chance to take master's-level education classes while still an undergrad. It was a lot — 18 credits, a full-time job, side hustles — but I was breathing. I was standing. I was alive. So I said yes.

That class? The one I was so nervous about because of what I allowed a professor to do to me? I got an A+. Not only that, I earned a letter of recommendation that opened real doors for me down the line. That one "yes" reshaped the rest of my path.

I eventually became a high school English teacher — and I loved it. Truly. Even with all the challenges I've written about, I wouldn't trade it. But even in those years of victory, the negative still found ways to whisper. You never fully silence it. But you *learn how to respond.*

One of the things I tell my students is this: *The Earth is going to spin on its axis, no matter what you're facing. Your job is to keep showing up.*

That's what I kept doing.

I started remembering who I was before the world got loud — a kid who walked home from the bus stop talking to birds, telling stories to trees. I didn't care how weird it looked. That was my joy. And somewhere along the way, I had given people power to make me feel small for that joy. I started living for their approval, not mine.

Losing my father changed that. Knowing he would never again see a sunset or hear the birds reminded me what a gift it is to be here. *To breathe. To exist.* I wanted to live from that place again — not just survive.

And for a while, I found that place again. I was happy. I was in nature, I was writing, I was teaching, I was *me.* But life doesn't stop. It moves, it tests, it spins. And I had to remember, again and again, how to flip the script.

Not everyone understands this mindset. We live in a world that sometimes confuses cynicism with intelligence. Some people see positivity as naïve, performative, even fake. I've had people say, *"You're always so positive— is that real?"* And I get it. I've been dismissed for not complaining. For smiling too often. For not "getting angry enough." That stings. Because what they don't understand is this: **positivity is my power.**

It's how I free myself from chains of doubt. It's how I heal. It's not performative. It's my resistance.

And when people don't get that? It's not personal. They're not ready. Or maybe they're still searching for their own light. And I've learned — I can't dim mine for their comfort.

And the truth is, I'm not everyone's cup of tea.

It took me a long time to accept that — longer still to celebrate it. But now I see it clearly. When people try to label me, dismiss me, or reduce me to a caricature, I realize it's not about *me*. It's about the lens they're stuck in. I used to shrink in those moments. Now I just breathe through them.

I stopped apologizing for being happy. For being hopeful. For believing in people. For believing in *myself.*

And that belief showed up again in one of the most unexpected ways — during the pandemic.

When the world shut down, we were left with ourselves. Some fell into fear. Some found purpose. For me, it was a bit of both. I started reconnecting with old practices — meditation, yoga, journaling. I had dabbled in those things for years, but now they became lifelines.

And through that time, I found a community. A tribe of women — creatives, spiritual seekers, lightworkers. We held space for one another. We laughed. We cried. We saw each other clearly. We reminded each other that we didn't have to perform to be accepted.

For the first time in a long time, I realized something quietly, slowly: I didn't have to *try* to be me. I could just *be*.

That realization began to shift how I showed up in every area of my life — especially with my students. I wasn't just the cheerleader for *them* anymore. I started becoming the cheerleader for *me* too.

That didn't make me selfish. It made me whole.

And in that wholeness, I started reclaiming dreams I had let sit in the background. Dreams I once talked about but never fully pursued. Among them? Screenwriting.

There was a story I had co-written with a partner. It had been sitting in the drawer of "maybe someday." During the pandemic, I submitted it — quietly, without telling him — to the 2nd Annual Stage 32 TV Pilot Drama Contest.

We made the quarterfinals. Then the semifinals. Then the finals.

And then… we won.

I flew to LA. I met producers, writers, people in the industry I'd admired from afar. And they told me — *your writing matters. Your characters feel real. Your voice is needed.*

My writing partner was thrilled — though, being a realist, he kept it grounded. But I was soaring. It felt like all the little pieces of me that had been waiting in the wings had finally stepped into the light.

Of course, life *lifes*.

Shortly after that, the industry was hit with a massive writers' strike. Everything paused. Meetings fell off. Momentum slowed.

And just like that, the noise came back---My negative voice---
*See? This is why you don't get too excited. It always ends. Who do
you think you are anyway?*

But this time... I didn't listen.

I let myself feel it — the frustration, the letdown, the ache. But it
didn't stop me. I kept writing. I *keep* writing. Because it's who I am.
Because it brings me back to joy.

And that's the thing: joy is never a waste. Hope is never a weakness.

Writing brings me joy. It brings me *home*. I'm still an educator,
still a mentor, still a guide. But I'm also a dreamer. A creator. And
that doesn't have to be put on pause for anyone — not even me.

I've been an educator for over two decades. I love mentoring. I love
championing students. But now I know: I must champion *myself*, too.
My dreams matter. My voice matters. I don't just want to *support*
creativity. I want to *embody* it.

So here I am.

Breathing. Writing. Living.

So, if you're wondering how to flip the script in your own life,
here's what I'll say:

No matter who doubts you, *you* get to believe. No matter how loud
the noise, *you* get to protect your peace. And even if the world doesn't
sip from your cup...

you still drink from it daily.

You still show up. You still shine. Flip the script. Sip your own tea.

✦ Reflection Questions – Chapter 4 ✦

Flipping the Script was all about reclaiming your power through perspective. This chapter explored what it means to face disappointment, burnout, and self-doubt—then choose to respond with resilience instead of retreat. This chapter peeled back the layers of what it means to "flip the script" on pain, limitations, and fear, showing that our greatest breakthroughs often come right after the moments we want to give up. Whether it was navigating a grueling schedule, surviving unexpected setbacks, or pushing forward in creative work despite silence or delay—it was meant to remind us that choosing to believe in ourselves is a daily act of courage. And that positivity is not naïve—it's a radical, conscious decision to live in hope.

Reflection Questions:

1. Think of a time when you faced a closed door or a setback. How did you respond? Did you choose to "flip the script" or fall into the negative story?

2. What recurring self-doubt narratives are keeping you stuck? Whose voice are they really?

3. What creative or personal dream have you quietly placed on pause? What one step could you take this week to pick it back up again?

Chapter FIVE

Finding Flow

Flow doesn't have to be constant to be real.

TRISH PERSEN

Chapter Five: Finding Flow

Flow doesn't have to be constant to be real.

As I'm sure you've known for a long time—whether you picked up this book after years of searching or stumbled across it when you needed it most—you didn't choose it by accident. We're drawn to certain stories, certain ideas, because something inside us is ready to hear them. We are seeking something, even if we're not yet sure what.

You've likely heard the word *flow* before. Being "in flow." It's more than a trend or a buzzword. Flow is a state of being—where the mind, body, and spirit align. Where there is no overthinking. No judgment. No fear. Just presence. Peace. Freedom.

In those moments, you're not trying to prove anything. You're not running from doubt or performing for approval. You're simply *being.* And you're more yourself in those moments than perhaps in any other.

I've experienced this state of flow throughout different chapters of my life—quiet, powerful moments where no outside influence could reach me, and I simply trusted. Trusted myself. Trusted the work. Trusted the journey.

One of the strongest examples of that came during a unit I created on poetry.

It always started the same way. I'd introduce the unit, and I'd hear it—one of those groans from the back of the classroom.

"Do we have to do a poetry unit?"

I'd laugh, every time. *"Oh, my dears—you think this unit is for you?"*

I'd pause. Let it land.
"This is my unit."

And I meant it. I had written it, built it, poured my soul into it. But the truth behind that smirk and sparkle in my voice was even deeper: this wasn't just my unit because I loved poetry.

It was mine because poetry saved me.

It carried me through heartbreak. Through grief. Through chapters where I had no idea who I was becoming or whether I would survive it. It was my voice when I couldn't speak, my rhythm when I couldn't stand, my truth when I couldn't be understood.

So yes, I built this unit. But my real goal wasn't to teach my students poetry.

It was to show them a mirror. To hand them a flashlight.
To help them meet themselves.

Poetry can feel intimidating or outdated, especially when we start with the classics. So I knew I had to bridge that gap. I attended retreats and workshops, and eventually, I found an educator teaching Hip Hop at the University of Miami. I lit up. I've always believed '90s hip hop artists were the street poets of our time.

That inspiration gave birth to the most transformative unit I'd ever taught.

My students resisted at first. They couldn't believe I expected them to write poems—*in English class!* I promised them, *"By the end of this unit, you'll be a writer."*

I created exercises that "tricked" them into experimenting with poetic forms. We'd open every class with one. They started as groans. Then they became guesses. Then curiosity. Then laughter. Then pride.

I paired classic poets with contemporary voices. Dickinson and J. Cole. Langston Hughes and Tupac. We made connections. We asked questions. We shared.

And I didn't just assign the work. I did it with them. Every challenge. Every poem. Every performance. We shared our musings aloud. We opened the classroom door and closed the rest of the world out.

We were in flow.

There was no judgment in that space. No comparison. Just us, our words, and our spirits—honest and present together.

And then—flow broke.

It always does. Because being in flow doesn't mean you stay in it forever.

You get tested. You get knocked down.

I remember it so clearly sitting at a table with soon-to-be colleagues, meant to welcome me and help me get acclimated. Let the awkward small talk commence. It started with the basics—where I was raised, where I went to school, what my degree was in.

I said I was from New York. That I had earned my English Literature degree from Molloy College.

You would've thought I told them I'd just been released from prison.

Two strikes. A "foreigner" from the North and a degree in literature—not education. I smiled through it. Said nothing. But later, I couldn't help but think—*You're discounting my English Literature degree… from teaching English Literature?*

You didn't ask about the 18 credits in education I took—on the master's level—while working full time and finishing my undergrad. You didn't ask how I passed state certification exams or why I chose this path at all.

I didn't bother to explain myself. I didn't need to.

Let them underestimate me. I'd let my work speak for itself.

That's the thing about flow. You learn how to return to it. You learn how to protect it. And you learn to stop giving your power away to people who never asked to understand you in the first place.

And the unit? It bloomed.

The most beautiful writing I'd ever seen came out of that classroom. Confidence took root. Students who once dreaded picking up a pencil found themselves creating spoken word, stanzas, and lyrics with pride. We became a community.

And I was a student again, too.

Because every time I taught that unit, I returned to myself.

Now—understand this: being in flow is not about perfection. And it isn't permanent. It's a practice. A choice. A homecoming. Sometimes you're in high-intensity flow—words flying, ideas landing, energy surging—and yet, the outside world won't move.

The industry might be slow. The inbox might be empty. Time might feel short.

But the creative part of you? The *real* you?

She's alive.

You just have to remember what she felt like.

One example is a creative partnership I had with a dear friend. The excitement was electric. Ideas kept coming. I planned, I organized

(Virgo energy in full effect), and we laid the groundwork for something meaningful.

But life lived. Priorities shifted. Energy waned.

And that's okay.

Not everything has to "happen" right away. The key is remembering what it felt like. How that high vibration fed your soul. Because if it brought joy once, it can again.

Flow doesn't have to be constant to be real.

Like I tell my students:
The Earth doesn't stop spinning just because you're struggling. So don't stop showing up.

You may not be someone's cup of tea right now. Or ever. But that's not your responsibility.

Let the tea leaves fall where they may. The right ones will be ready to sip. The others can brew their own.

✦ Reflection Questions – Chapter 5 ✦

Finding Flow revealed the quiet power that comes when you allow yourself to simply be—unapologetically, creatively, and wholly. This chapter reminded us that flow isn't a constant state, but a return-to-self we must nurture. Whether through poetry, performance, or teaching, in my personal case, flow is where authenticity meets action. It's in the moments where the noise fell away, and presence took over—where your gifts aligned with your purpose. A reminder that although life's responsibilities and doubts may interrupt that state, we always have the power to reconnect with what lights us up. Flow isn't about perfection—it's about presence, joy, and honoring what makes us feel most alive.

Reflection Questions:

1. When was the last time you felt completely in flow—present, creative, and at peace? What were you doing?

2. What interrupts your flow most often—external pressures or internal doubts?

3. In what spaces of your life do you feel most like yourself? How can you spend more time in those spaces?

4. Think about a time you dimmed your light to fit in. What did you learn from that experience?

Chapter SIX

Not everyone will clap for you

There's a quiet peace in that shift. A freedom.

TRISH PERSEN

Chapter Six: Not everyone will clap for you.

There's a quiet peace in that shift. A freedom.

Realizing that not everyone will clap for you was a hard, unexpected lesson—one I didn't see coming until it hit me square in the heart. I had spent so much of my life showing up for others—supporting, cheering, mentoring, and holding space. I assumed, almost innocently, that the love I gave would return to me in kind. That when my moment came, there'd be thunderous applause echoing back. But sometimes, there is silence. And sometimes, silence speaks louder than applause ever could.

At first, that realization hurt. Deeply.

It felt like betrayal—like all the energy, all the joy I'd poured into others had disappeared into a void. I wrestled with questions that left bruises: Was I naive? Did they never really care? Was I not worthy of the same love I gave away so freely?

But here's what I've come to understand: when you begin to truly find your way—when your light shines a little brighter and your truth grows a little louder—not everyone will want to celebrate that. Not because they don't care. Sometimes it's because they don't know how to hold space for your becoming, especially when they're still unsure of their own.

It's not always jealousy or malice. Sometimes, it's fear.

Other times, it's a mirror.

When you evolve, when you rise, when you step into your own flow, it can reflect the places others feel stuck or small or unseen. Your growth becomes a light—and light, while beautiful, can be blinding.

Still, it stings. Especially when it comes from the people you love most. You think those who've known you the longest—family, lifelong friends, even colleagues you've stood beside for years—will be your biggest cheerleaders. But blood, time, and proximity don't guarantee support. That was a hard pill to swallow.

And yet, it's an essential one.

Because if you're constantly waiting for applause, for permission, or for validation, you'll stay stuck. You'll clip your own wings trying to fit into the image someone else has of you. You'll spend your energy managing perception instead of living your purpose.

I know this because I've done it.

I remember vividly the first time I chose not to share an accomplishment out loud. I had been given the opportunity to pursue a second Master's degree in creative writing. The tuition was covered through my career—a rare, precious chance to chase a dream without the weight of debt. It should've been a joyful moment, one I shouted from rooftops.

But instead, I whispered it only to my husband.

We had a long talk about what it would mean. The time. The pressure. The balance of work, side hustles, and now, school. But together, we agreed: *Let's do it.* He believed in me without hesitation. But beyond our four walls, I didn't breathe a word.

Why?

Because something inside me told me it wouldn't be received with excitement. I didn't want to hear *"Again?"* or *"Another degree?"* said with that tone—half-dismissive, half-resentful. I didn't want to make excuses when I had to miss a dinner or couldn't be as present at a party. So I showed up to everything anyway, never letting on how exhausted I was. I celebrated everyone else, even as I quietly juggled a second full-time job in the form of grad school.

And it hurts.

It hurt to feel like I had to hide something that meant so much to me. It hurts that the idea of my progress could make people uncomfortable. And it hurt that I had started to anticipate silence instead of celebration.

But the biggest realization—the one that changed everything—was this:

It wasn't their job to clap for me.

It wasn't anyone's responsibility to validate my path or understand the depth of my ambition. That job belonged to me. And when I didn't get the reaction I wanted, it wasn't their failure—it was my own expectation setting me up for disappointment.

I was the one reacting to their reactions.

That's when it clicked. The disappointment I was feeling didn't start with them—it started with me. I had given away the power to affirm myself. I had let the absence of clapping become a commentary on my worth.

And once I saw that, I could start to reclaim it.

I no longer needed loud cheers. I didn't need the grand, showy affirmations. I just needed to remember why I started—to remember that I didn't go back for that degree to impress anyone. I did it because it was mine. Because writing is my oxygen. Because I had stories living inside me that deserved to breathe.

Still, I won't pretend it was easy. I'm a giver by nature. I love celebrating others, lifting them up, throwing the party, clapping the loudest. I do that because I know what it's like to feel invisible. I've always wanted to make others feel seen, especially the ones who rarely are. But sometimes, I gave so much that I forgot to hold any celebration for myself.

So when the clapping stopped—or when it never started—I didn't know what to do with the quiet.

Eventually, I realized: I had to be my own applause.

I had to clap for myself. Loudly. On purpose. Without shame.

Because sometimes the silence is just a test: a test of how deeply you believe in your own magic when no one else is watching.

That moment was a turning point. I had to ask myself: *Why do I do what I do? Who is it really for?*

If the answer wasn't me—my soul, my joy, my calling—then it was time to recalibrate.

I'm still the same person who plans the surprise parties, who writes poems for others on their birthdays, who remembers the little things and shows up big. That hasn't changed. What has changed is that I don't expect it to come back in the same way. I give because I love. But I no longer give to prove I'm worthy of being loved in return.

There's a quiet peace in that shift. A freedom.

I still get my feelings hurt from time to time—don't we all? But I don't spiral anymore. I don't interpret silence as an attack or lack of recognition as rejection. I take note, I adjust my boundaries, and I keep it moving. Because I know who I am. I know what I bring. I know what I've overcome to be here.

And if someone else can't see that?

It's okay. I do.

So maybe you're reading this with a lump in your throat, remembering a time someone didn't clap for you when you needed it most. Maybe it was a best friend, a parent, a partner, a sibling.

Maybe it was someone you've always shown up for, someone you believed would do the same for you.

Let me tell you what I've learned: it's not about them.

This is your life, your art, your journey. You get to decide what's worth celebrating. You get to choose what deserves your energy. You get to write your story—not based on their applause, but on your own knowing.

Celebrate anyway.

Clap anyway.

Create anyway.

Keep showing up for yourself even when the room is quiet. Because eventually, the right people will hear your rhythm—and they'll clap because they truly see you, not because they feel obligated to.

And until then? ----You'll be enough. Always.

Not everyone will clap for you.

That realization stings more when the silence comes from people you expected to celebrate with—family, lifelong friends, even colleagues you've championed. But this chapter reminded us that not all applause is meant for every stage of your journey, and that's okay. The deeper truth is this: your worth, your victories, your creative joy—none of it depends on someone else's cheers. This chapter wasn't just about disappointment; it was about reclaiming your voice, validating your own path, and recognizing the difference between seeking support and depending on it. When we learn to clap for ourselves, even in the quiet, we gain the kind of strength that sustains us through the highs and the heartbreaks. You don't need a room full of approval to shine. You only need to stand in your truth.

Reflection Questions

1. Have you ever felt the absence of support from someone you deeply expected to show up for you? How did it affect you—and how did you move forward?

2. When you experience a win or a personal achievement, who are the first people you turn to? What happens when they don't respond the way you hoped?

3. Are there any relationships in your life where you feel you're constantly giving without receiving? What boundaries might help protect your energy? What would it look like to clap for yourself—without apology, without waiting for permission?

Chapter SEVEN

Owning Your Narrative

Nobody else can write your story.

TRISH PERSEN

Chapter Seven: Owning Your Narrative

Nobody else can write your story.

The power of owning your own narrative is profound. But it doesn't happen overnight. It arrives only after you've stumbled through countless shadows, after you've felt lost in your own life. We all experience times when we feel like life is just happening to us—when we're merely reacting, absorbing what others say, letting the outside world define what's true.

Deflection becomes a way of surviving. If I don't acknowledge this thing—this pain, this failure, this fear—then maybe it isn't real. Maybe it'll pass on its own. We do this because ownership feels like a verdict, a stamp of permanence. And if what's in front of us is bad—really bad—owning it feels like surrendering to it. So we spiral. We tell ourselves stories: this will never feel peaceful, this will never be okay.

Or on the flip side—when things are good, truly good—we question it, too. We wonder how long the joy will last, how long the success will stay. Can I trust this? Can I really lean into this happiness? It's wild how we're more comfortable doubting ourselves than embracing joy. But the truth is: none of us know how long something will last. And trying to predict it won't make it stay.

What we can control—what we absolutely *must* control—is how we respond. That's where our power lies. That's where we start writing our own narrative.

I know I talk about this a lot in these chapters, but it's not repetition—it's rhythm. Life is made of these cycles. That ebb and flow of being knocked down and choosing to get back up again, of silencing the noise and deciding that *you* are the author of your story. No one else. People will try—oh, they will try—to write it for you. They'll make assumptions. They'll narrate your life through their lens, their projections, their biases. But they don't get that right. They don't get to tell you who you are.

You do.

That truth is something I've had to rediscover again and again, through different chapters of my life. And for me, that rediscovery almost always begins with a blank page. Since I was a child, I've turned to notebooks and journals like lifeboats. My mom—a beautiful writer herself—taught me how to turn even spelling words into poetry. Instead of writing dry sentences with our weekly word list, she helped me craft stanzas, little vignettes, even if they didn't follow all the "rules." It was magic. It gave me permission to be expressive in a world that didn't always make room for that.

I was a quiet, mousy kid. Small. Shy. Always observing. Never the loudest in the room. Physically, I was often in specialized classes due to challenges with coordination and balance—things I wouldn't fully understand until later in life. But emotionally? Spiritually? I was soaking everything in. And what I couldn't say out loud, I wrote. Or danced. Or played through my saxophone in band. I communicated through movement and music and metaphor. That was my language.

But middle school—that time between innocence and identity—was brutal. It felt like overnight, people forgot how to be kind. Suddenly, being different became a target. You didn't need a reason to be disliked. I was told, "You know when you just don't like someone?" And that was it. No explanation. No justice. Just quiet cruelty.

It made me shrink even smaller. I second-guessed everything. I became afraid to be seen. I told myself I was safest in the background. But even then—even in that isolation—I began to feel a quiet resistance building inside me. I didn't have the experience to fully articulate it, but something in me knew I didn't have to live like this forever. There *was* a different way to be.

And for me, that came from finding peace and friendship outside the four walls of school. In my neighborhood, I had a group of friends who weren't caught up in the social hierarchy. We could be weird. We could be loud or quiet. We could make up stories and act out ridiculous scenes and be exactly who we were. That contrast—the chaos of school and the calm of my little tribe—taught me that *I* had the power to choose where to place my energy. I could choose peace. I could choose joy.

Still, the ache of middle school lingered. It was a kind of mourning, a sadness I carried deep into high school. Until one unexpected friendship rewrote everything.

It started in 10th grade, in journalism class. There was a student in the room who looked familiar, but different. Long hair. Painted nails. A boldness in how he carried himself that I admired instantly. And then it clicked—this was Freddy.

Freddy, who once—back in first grade—ripped a doll from my arms and tore it apart. A doll my godmother had sewn just for me. One of the few dolls I had that looked like *me*—brown hair, brown eyes, a reflection I rarely saw. I remember the devastation, the humiliation. That day left a scar.

But here we were, years later, reintroduced under new light. And instead of bitterness, something else bloomed between us. We connected over poetry, over sarcasm, over late-90s angst. We laughed. We supported each other. We created together.

And slowly, the scar healed.

Not once did I bring up the doll. I didn't need to. The person standing in front of me now—the one encouraging me to take drama class with him, the one helping me find my voice—wasn't the same boy who once tore something from my hands. He was something far more powerful: someone who saw me. Who respected me. Who believed in me when I still struggled to believe in myself.

He told me, "You have so much heart. So much love. So much to offer. One day, Trish, you're going to be on top. Remember that."

And I did. I still do.

That friendship changed everything. It helped me step into myself. I started speaking up. Performing. Taking risks. Becoming. And the most beautiful part of all of it was that we never labeled anything. There were no boxes. No pronouns. No expectations. Freddy was just… Freddy. And I loved him for that.

But here's the thing—life doesn't always give us fairytale endings.

One of the last conversations we had before summer break was him confiding in me that he wanted to dress how he truly wanted at graduation. He worried his father wouldn't come. I told him he should do it anyway. That he was beautiful. That those who loved him would see him.

His father didn't come.

That summer, we didn't see each other as much. Life was busy. Money was tight. We kept in touch, but the days slipped by. Until one day, I got a call. Freddy's brother had found him.

You already know what that means.

There are no words that can fully hold what I felt in that moment. It crushed me. It still does. And I debated whether to include this story here. But I am. Because if you're reading this, and you've ever questioned your worth, or your voice, or your right to take up space—please listen:

Nobody else can heal you.
Nobody else can write your story.
You have to do that for yourself.

Yes, find your people. Yes, open your heart to love and friendship. But *do not* let the outside noise be louder than your own voice. Freddy gave me courage. He helped me find my light. But he couldn't see his own. And I wish—God, I wish—I could have helped him carry that.

So this chapter is for Freddy. And for anyone who has ever felt like they weren't allowed to be who they are. Who's been told—through words or silence—that they don't belong. ---You do.

Owning your narrative means you get to decide how your story goes. Yes, there are other characters—mentors, antagonists, background noise—but you are the *protagonist*. You decide who has power. You decide who gets the mic. You decide what chapters are worth writing---write them.

Write the messy ones. The healing ones. The ones where you don't know what's next but you show up anyway. Let your story be yours—even when it's misunderstood. Especially when it's misunderstood. Because someone will see you. And more importantly, you'll see *yourself*.

✦ Reflection Questions – Chapter 7 ✦

The power of owning your narrative is one of the most courageous acts of self-love. In this chapter, we journeyed through the raw, formative spaces where you first began to understand that your story is yours to tell—and yours alone. We looked back at my childhood silences, middle school isolation, and the unlikely friendship that helped me come back to myself. We explored how others may try to define you through labels, assumptions, or even absence, but your voice—however quiet at first—was always there, waiting for you to listen. Taking authorship of your own life isn't about rewriting the hard parts; it's about claiming the whole journey, including the darkness that shaped your light. This chapter reminded us that we get to choose how our stories unfold—and that's where the real transformation begins.

Reflection Questions

1. In what ways have you allowed others to write or define your story—either through their words, actions, or silence?

2. Can you recall a moment when someone helped you see yourself more clearly or reminded you of your worth?

3. Where in your life are you still afraid to speak up or take ownership of your truth?

4. What narrative from your past do you need to revisit—not to relive it, but to reclaim it?

5. How would your life shift if you truly believed you were the author of your own story?

Chapter EIGHT

Pour From Your Own Cup

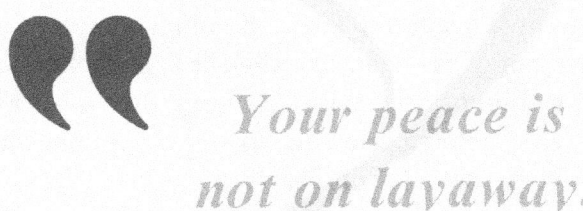

*Your peace is
not on layaway.*

TRISH PERSEN

Chapter Eight: Pour From Your Own Cup

Your peace is not on layaway.

You've heard it before: *You can't pour from an empty cup.* And while it may sound cliché, take a moment and really picture it. Imagine tipping that cup as far as it can go, angling it in every direction, shaking it, hoping—pleading—that something will come out. But it doesn't. Because it's empty. There is nothing left.

That's what it's like when we try to give from a place of depletion. When we ignore our own needs and keep extending ourselves, again and again, until our energy has been stretched so thin it's threadbare. If the liquid in that metaphorical cup is our energy, then the act of pouring—loving, giving, helping, showing up—is impossible when we haven't taken time to replenish ourselves.

And yet, so many of us do just that. We give, not because we have anything to spare, but because we believe we *should*. Because we want to be accepted. Because we think it will make someone else happy. Because we want to be seen, to be included. We pour, not from overflow, but from obligation. From guilt. From the hope that maybe, if we just give a little more, we'll finally be enough.

That's where this chapter begins: with the realization that we must stop pouring from an empty cup—especially when we're doing it for people who will never be satisfied. People who may never clap for us. People for whom we will never be "just right."

It's okay not to be their cup of tea. And it's more than okay to stop offering sips from your own soul in hopes of winning them over.

The truth is, this has been the theme all along—this entire journey has been about reclaiming energy. Realizing that sometimes, we keep ourselves stuck not because of others, but because of ourselves. Because we're the ones who keep showing up for people who stopped showing up for us a long time ago.

You can only begin to conserve your energy once you see things clearly—not through the lens of old stories, wounds, or expectations, but through the truth of your lived experience. And the truth is this: joy and peace are choices. Sometimes hard ones. But they are always within reach.

I know this isn't easy. I am not naive. Sometimes the weight of the world doesn't just sit on our shoulders—it pins us to the ground. There are moments when anxiety clutches our chest, when fear steals our breath, when darkness surrounds us so tightly it feels suffocating. Sometimes joy feels like a lie. Sometimes the "cup" feels shattered entirely.

But even then, we have a choice. Do we stay in that space, or do we fight for our light?

Reclaiming your energy starts by making room for your own joy—even the smallest joys. For me, that's sitting on my back porch, which opens to a quiet nature preserve. It's the sunrise stretching across the sky. The birds singing their own greeting to the day. It's taking care of my plants. Walking on the beach. Watching the moonrise. None of these things cost a dime, but they feed my soul. They fill my cup.

And that's the difference between surviving and thriving.

The world wants you to believe that joy comes from the big things—vacations, promotions, the right outfit, the perfect body, the fancy dinner on a yacht in Santorini. But the real secret? It's found in simplicity.

Because when you can find joy in what's already within your reach, you stop chasing. You stop comparing. You stop believing that happiness lives in the land of *"once I have…"* and *"when I get…"*

Once I get the job, then I'll be happy.
Once I'm married, then I'll feel whole.
Once I finish the degree, once I buy the house, once I lose the weight, then…

That's the trap. Because the truth is, once you get that thing, it fades. The high dissipates. And you find yourself reaching again for the next thing. The next cup. The next drop of approval or proof that you are worthy.

Stop the cycle. Step out of the loop.

Your peace is not on layaway. You don't need to earn it. You don't need to chase it. It lives within you.

And it's your job to protect it.

Let me tell you a story that changed me.

Her name was Barbara. She was older than me, probably by a couple of decades. We first saw her near a strip of abandoned storefronts in a shopping center—not unusual in Florida, but what was unusual was Barbara herself. She lived there. She had her shopping cart, yoga mats, blankets, a setup that looked like a space she chose, not one forced upon her.

What struck me wasn't just that she was unhoused—it was that people treated her like a problem to be solved. They'd crouch down to her like she was a child, offer her food like she should be grateful for scraps. She refused most of it. And you could tell, it wasn't out of pride—it was because the energy felt off. Condescending. Performative.

One night near Christmas, my husband and I stopped by the shopping center to pick up something for our nephew. Barbara was there. I had that moment—the one where you hesitate. *Should I approach? Will she want to be bothered?* But something in me said go. So I sat down beside her on the curb and introduced myself.

"Hi, I'm Trish," I said. She smiled. "You're from New York, huh?"

The accent gave me away.

We talked. We laughed. She was dressed in this flowing gown, hair done, energy serene. She told me she was a mother, a former activist, a professional. She had lived a full, colorful life. And now, she chose freedom. No strings. No expectations. Just peace.

I asked if I could buy her a coffee, and she reached into her basket for her wallet. She insisted on paying. "I got this," she said. And I saw the power in her eyes.

Barbara wasn't sad. She wasn't lacking. She wasn't broken. She was living a life most people wouldn't understand. But she understood it. And that was enough.

When we brought her coffee back, she gave a small smile, sipped, and gave the universal *okay* hand gesture. Content. Whole. Replenished.

Barbara was a lesson. A reminder that you create your own reality. That peace is yours to define. That joy is not one-size-fits-all.

It reminded me, too, of how far we've come as a species—and how much we've forgotten. Our ancestors survived by gathering, sharing stories, sitting around fires, dancing beneath stars. Joy wasn't transactional. It was communal. It was rooted in presence, in being alive, in weathering storms together.

We don't need more *things*. We need more presence. More listening. More moments where we step away from the screens and the schedules and the scarcity mindsets to ask ourselves: *What fills my cup?*

Because until you can answer that, you will keep pouring from a place of emptiness. You'll keep trying to earn joy instead of living in it.

So today, my friend, I ask you:

What fills you up?
What replenishes your energy?
What makes you breathe easier, smile wider, sleep deeper?

Go there. Do that. Drink deeply.

Because when you fill your own cup, you don't just have more to give—you give with joy, not resentment. You create from wholeness, not exhaustion. You live in alignment, not performance.

Fill your cup. Then let it overflow—not to be accepted, not to prove anything, but because joy, when shared, multiplies.

You can't pour from an empty cup—and yet so many of us try, again, and again until we're running on fumes. This chapter gently but powerfully reminded us that joy is not selfish, rest is not laziness, and self-replenishment is not optional. Through simple moments of mindfulness, connection, and presence—from birdsong and moonrises to heartfelt conversations with a woman named Barbara—we're shown that fulfillment often lives in the small, quiet choices we make every day. The truth is: your energy is sacred. Protecting it doesn't make you less generous—it ensures you can continue to give in a way that's authentic and sustainable. When you start drinking from your own reservoir, you no longer depend on external validation or extravagant circumstances to feel whole. You remember that peace is created, not found.

Reflection Questions

1. What are the small, everyday things that truly fill your cup?

2. How do you recognize when your emotional or spiritual energy is running low?

3. In what ways have you been overextending yourself in hopes of being accepted or seen?

4. What would it look like to give yourself permission to rest, even if nothing is "finished"?

5. Who or what inspires you to slow down and replenish—without guilt?

Chapter NINE

Owning your Message

*Preach what
you practice*

TRISH PERSEN

Chapter Nine: Owning your Message

Preach what you practice

We've all heard the phrase *"practice what you preach."* It's been instilled in me for as long as I can remember—like some kind of moral compass we're expected to carry. But lately, I've been thinking about it in reverse: *Preach what you practice.*

This entire book has been a process of reflection. It's been about finding clarity in my own power, about realizing—truly accepting—that I am not everyone's cup of tea. And that's okay.

But what good is this hard-earned insight if I keep it to myself?

I've learned that I'm not alone in this discovery. So many people out there may not yet have the words for it, but they've felt the ache of not being someone's favorite. They've tried to shift themselves into something more "palatable," only to lose touch with who they really are. Especially in the arts. Especially in the entertainment industry. Especially in life.

In my role as an educator—specifically teaching communications at a university that caters to students breaking into arts and entertainment—this theme surfaces all the time. My students are creators, performers, dreamers. They're also fragile. Unformed, uncertain, trying to discover where they fit and, more often, where they don't.

One of the most transformative discussions we have is on **personal branding**. The room usually goes quiet when I bring it up—not because the term is foreign, but because its implications are heavy. I'll walk around the room, reading their unease before they even speak.

"You already have a personal brand," I tell them. "You've been branded since birth."

They blink. That's not what they expected to hear.

But it's true. Whether we realize it or not, we've been cultivating and projecting a version of ourselves all our lives. And in the entertainment industry especially, your brand is rarely just about *you*. It's about perception. It's about how others receive and interpret your energy, your voice, your message.

That can be terrifying. Cue the *oh no* moment: *"You mean I'm being judged… all the time?"*

Yes. But that's not the point. The point is: **you have power in how you show up.**

When I first introduced the phrase *"You're not everyone's cup of tea, and that's okay"* in class, I didn't expect it to resonate the way it did. I thought I was just saying something to soften the edges of a difficult topic. But I saw the impact immediately. It stuck. They were leaning in. They were finally breathing.

It gave them permission. Permission to stop striving for approval from audiences that will never clap for them. Permission to direct their energy toward the ones who will.

Because here's the thing—when students start building their brands, they often dream of being *everything to everyone*. It's well-meaning. It comes from a genuine desire to connect, to make an impact. But "everyone" is not a real audience. And trying to reach "everyone" is a fast track to burnout and identity crisis.

I've had students write their branding pitches with phrases like "My audience is everyone!" And I get it. I understand the sentiment. But I ask them to dig deeper. Who are they really speaking to? Who lights up when they speak, sing, paint, act, or write? Who is their message meant for?

This is where the *cup of tea* concept becomes real. We're not for everyone. We're not *supposed* to be. And just as we don't vibe with every artist, brand, or voice we come across—others won't vibe with us. And that's not rejection. That's redirection. That's clarity.

This realization changes how my students approach not just their careers, but their self-worth.

In our modern world, where everything is shared and everything is seen, it can feel like we're all living on a stage. Social media has collapsed the distance between our private lives and public personas. Suddenly, we know too much. The mystique is gone. And with that, comes critique—instant, relentless, and often misinformed.

So what do we do? How do we protect ourselves and still show up?

We root ourselves in purpose.

I tell my students: *Find your tribe. Find your true audience.* Because you might have only ten people in a room. But if those ten people are changed by what you create—if they see you, hear you, and grow from your message—that is impact. That is purpose. That is legacy.

Success isn't always about scaling. Sometimes it's about *sustaining*. Sometimes your audience is small, but sacred.

And what about the critics? What about the opposition?

Let them exist. We need opposition. We need differing views and clashing opinions because they help sharpen our clarity. They push us to define what matters most. It's okay if someone doesn't like what you do. It doesn't mean you're not talented. It doesn't mean you're not worthy.

It just means they're not your audience.

There was a time when I took every blank stare, every bit of indifference in the classroom, personally. I was trying to win everyone over. I wanted every student to walk away with a spark. And while many did—some didn't. Some wouldn't. And I had to learn to be okay with that.

What I *can* control is how I show up. I show up consistently. Authentically. With heart and purpose. That's how I teach. That's how I live. That's how I brand myself.

And that's what I preach.

So when my students feel discouraged because they didn't go viral, or because one professor didn't "get" them, or because their audience isn't growing fast enough—I remind them that their message will reach *who it's meant to reach.*

Your only job is to stay aligned with your values, your voice, your truth.

You're not everyone's cup of tea. And that's more than okay.

✦ Reflection Questions – Chapter 9 ✦

In this chapter, we beautifully closed the loop—taking the personal journey of self-discovery and applying it outward, into your role as an educator and guide. "You're not everyone's cup of tea—and that's okay" became more than a mantra; it became a tool for mentorship, for empowerment, and for helping others shape their own narratives. Through teaching personal branding to emerging artists and creatives, you're reminding your students—and yourself—that we all carry a message, but not all messages are meant for everyone. That truth is not rejection; it's redirection. It's freedom. To pay it forward is to walk in authenticity while creating space for others to do the same. It's about modeling what it looks like to believe in yourself even when the room is quiet—and helping others learn to do that too.

Reflection Questions

1. In what ways have you shared the lessons you've learned with others in your life or work?

2. What message are you sending to the world through your actions, presence, or creative work?

3. How do you support others in owning their stories—without shrinking your own?

4. What does "audience" mean to you in your personal or professional life? Are you reaching the people you're meant to?

5. If you could teach one truth to someone coming behind you, what would it be?

Chapter TEN
NO explanation needed

People will always speak from their own lens.

TRISH PERSEN

Chapter 10: NO explanation needed.

People will always speak from their own lens.

The shit people say often makes us feel as though we have to defend ourselves. For some reason, we feel like because we don't satisfy a quote-unquote answer that fits into their reality—or what they believe life is supposed to look like—we owe them a reaction. We scramble to satisfy a truth that doesn't belong to us.

Now, don't get me wrong: most people say things not out of malice, but because they're caught up in the same cycles. They speak from the perception of how things "should" be, based on a model of life they never really questioned. And so they say things, without much thought, unaware that their words land in our spirit as wounds.

What happens is we get caught. Caught internalizing all of it. Absorbing it as though it's a personal attack. And maybe it should feel that way. But if we come at it from the understanding that, no matter what we do, we're not going to be everyone's cup of tea—and we're okay with that—then we can walk away from these conversations with grace. We can take them with a grain of salt, knowing that the commentary says more about them than it does about us.

You've heard the cliché: assumptions make an ass out of you and me. And yet we live in a world full of them.

Let's say you're a woman in your late twenties or thirties. No child in sight. You're at a theme park with your significant other, just the two of you. And here it comes, like a reflex:

"Oh, you don't have kids?"

That lifted tone at the end, as if it's a question cloaked in curiosity but wrapped in judgment. Like somehow your reality doesn't add up. Like you've skipped a step. Like you must be broken—or worse, selfish.

They don't know what's behind the question. They don't know what it unearths.

At first, I'd answer passively. "We're just not ready yet." I'd smile. I'd deflect. If it was a stranger or someone I'd never see again, it was easier to detach. But when it came from students—kids I'd taught and mentored—it was harder. They'd say things like:

"Mrs. P, you'd be such a great mom."
"You'd be the best."

And I'd smile, again. "Oh, I'm a super auntie. And I love what I do." I'd deflect again. But inside? Inside, it was painful.

Because what they didn't know—and didn't need to know—was that I had lived through the confusion of misdiagnosed endometriosis for years. I had experienced the quiet trauma of miscarriages I didn't even recognize as miscarriages. I had been told over and over that my pain was normal, that once I had a baby, I'd be "cured." That everything would be fine.

So I believed that story. I let others write that chapter of my life.

Until 2008.

It was supposed to be a celebratory year. I was the sponsor of the class of 2008—the same students I had mentored from freshmen to seniors. I loved them deeply. But that spring, the pain came back stronger. I dismissed it. "It's just my endometriosis," I told myself. "I'll push through."

But it didn't pass. I couldn't even stand. I was teaching from a chair, barely making it through the day. Finally, I went back to my doctor and demanded to be seen. Blood tests. Pale face. And then—the big smile. The congratulations. The doctor actually hugged me.

"You're pregnant."

But I knew. I knew in my bones that something wasn't right. Still, I let him tell me how I should feel. He handed me vitamins. Gave me a plan. Called it a blessing.

There was no heartbeat. Weeks passed. The devastation confirmed what my body already knew. I went through a D&C, and it was there that I learned the truth—that I had already miscarried before. Multiple times.

Even in all that pain, I still allowed others to narrate my story. I deferred to their version of what I was going through. I silenced my truth to make others comfortable.

But here's what I know now: **You don't owe anyone an explanation.**

Especially not for the shape of your life, the way your timeline unfolds, or the path you walk. People will always speak from their own lens. They'll always question what they don't understand. It doesn't mean they're evil. It just means they're writing a story in their heads based on societal handcuffs that no longer fit.

You don't need to explain why your family doesn't look like theirs. Why your life isn't happening in the "order" they expected. Why are you childfree, or divorced, or single, or starting over—again.

Let them wonder. Let them sip from their own cups. Keep yours.

✦ Reflection Questions – Chapter 10 ✦

This chapter is your permission slip. To no longer explain. To no longer justify your timeline, your decisions, or your pain. Not everyone will understand your story—and they don't need to. The pressure to explain comes from an outdated idea that we need others to approve of our lives in order to live them fully. But the truth is: your life belongs to you.

And while some questions may come from ignorance, not cruelty, that doesn't mean they deserve a chapter of your soul in response. Your story is sacred. Guard it with intention. You are enough. Your path is enough. You don't owe anyone an explanation.

Reflection Questions

1. How have you felt pressure to explain yourself in the past, especially when your path didn't match societal expectations?

2. What stories have you allowed others to write for you—and are you ready to reclaim authorship?

3. How do you respond (internally or externally) when people ask questions that feel invasive or presumptive?

4. What truths have you carried quietly that deserve to be honored, not justified?

5. How can you practice setting gentle, firm boundaries when people project their expectations onto you?

Afterword

So, you're not everyone's cup of tea.

TRISH PERSEN

Afterword

You weren't brewed for their comfort.

So, you're not everyone's cup of tea.

We've established that by now—maybe they prefer coffee. Maybe they're into sparkling water, oat milk lattes, or something stronger. Whatever the case, the real question is: *Why do we even care?* Why do we spend so much of our time and energy worrying whether or not our particular blend of soul and spirit is palatable to someone else?

Why do we pour ourselves into chasing acceptance, contorting ourselves into shapes we were never meant to hold, just to make someone else comfortable? We wrap our daily lives in this pursuit, often without realizing it's not even *our* happiness we're chasing—it's a mirage of it. A version built on validation and external approval, rather than truth.

What I've learned—and what I truly hope you've discovered through these pages—is that we *do* have the power to shift that mindset. Every single day, we get to choose how we show up. We get to decide whose opinions get to take up space in our minds, whose energy is allowed to influence ours, and what reality we want to live in. That control is ours. It's always been ours.

People will craft their own stories. That's human nature. They will form opinions, draw conclusions, and project expectations. But those stories belong to them—not to you.

No one else gets to define your value, your worth, or your strength. No one knows the battles you've fought just to bloom, or how many storms you've weathered just to still be standing. Only you know what it's taken to be here now reading these words, breathing this breath.

And that's sacred.

I'll admit, it's taken me a long time to get to this space of clarity. I'm not some wise old sage sitting atop a mountain—I'm just a woman approaching mid-century, who's finally realized that energy is too precious to waste on proving myself to anyone who's not ready to receive me. My time is my own, and how I'm perceived is not my problem.

That's a hard-earned truth, but one I hold close now. We all have our preferences—our cups, our brews, our rituals. Just like I need my coffee a certain way each morning, some people will want you to show up a certain way to suit their taste. If you don't, they'll wrinkle their nose, pour you out, and move on.

Let them. You weren't brewed for their comfort.

This entire book has been about discovering your truth, reclaiming your power, and learning to show up as yourself—without apology. Every story has been a piece of my journey. The stumbling, the questioning, the failing, the rediscovery—it's all here. And through it all, one truth has remained constant: I may not be everyone's cup of tea, but that's okay. Because not everyone is *mine* either.

And that's a beautiful thing.

We're not supposed to be the same. We weren't created to mirror each other's paths. What a dull world it would be if we were. The brilliance of humanity is in its diversity—of thought, of experience, of energy. We're not all brewed from the same leaf, and we're not meant to steep in the same teapot.

I believe, in my soul, that we are all created by something greater than ourselves. We each carry a spark of the Divine, whatever form that takes for you. To deny someone's existence, someone's identity, someone's way of being—because it doesn't align with your comfort—is, to me, a disservice to that spark. A denial of the very divinity that created us all.

You were made as you are for a reason.

You don't need to be anyone else's idea of enough. You already are. You don't need to force yourself into spaces that ask you to shrink. You weren't born to fit molds—you were born to break them.

So let go.

Let go of the pressure to prove.
Let go of the need to be liked by everyone.
Let go of the stories that were never yours to begin with.

And instead—sip from your own cup.

Fill it with the things that bring you peace. Fill it with joy, with reflection, with songs that make you dance barefoot in your kitchen. Fill it with laughter, with real conversations, with mornings that feel like new chances and nights that feel like rest. Fill it with your *self*—the you who's always been waiting to be fully seen, fully heard, fully loved.

And then drink deeply.

Because you, my friend, are the perfect cup of tea.

For you.

And that is more than enough.

You can access all my social and contacts here:

Also Available: Shift-Your-Narrative-28-Days

https://a.co/d/bkGLz6P

New Project Coming Soon: Children's Book

www.ingramcontent.com/pod-product-compliance
Lightning Source LLC
Chambersburg PA
CBHW061656120626
46550CB00003B/970